T0208646

THOUGHTS
of
LIFE

Matthew Grunder

authorHOUSE®

AuthorHouse™
1663 Liberty Drive
Bloomington, IN 47403
www.authorhouse.com
Phone: 833-262-8899

Published by AuthorHouse 05/31/2022

ISBN: 978-1-6655-5723-8 (sc)
ISBN: 978-1-6655-5724-5 (e)

Library of Congress Control Number: 2022907399

CONTENTS

IT COMMUNICATION
written by: Matthew Grunder
September 16, 2009

"I" to the "T"
in the
Seabee
Navy.
When out to sea,
no one communicates
better than me.
I got circuits, ADP,
and message traffic.
Watch out terrorists I'll reek havoc.
Anything you send my way,
ain't nothing going down today.
All comms are here to stay.
And here some more I got to say.
"We control the switches, the tables
and the cables.
Without that, you just aren't able.
You can talk about us,
but you can't talk without us.
So don't fuss if you cannot hear.
We must stop all acts of fear,
and celebrate with beer."

CORPORATION DEPRIVATION

written by Matthew Grunder
February 23, 2011

Corporation
part of organization
created the operation
to the creation
of the infestation
for all frustration.

Instigation.

Call police station,
fire station,
and government federation
to use specialization.

Launch the investigation
on the administration
using all communication
to find the information
about the criminalization.

Start by alphabetization
to find correlation
of characterization.

Confirmation.

Make duplication
of the documentation
showing location.

Issue the citation
of violation
explaining legalization.

Hesitation.
There goes reputation.
Better make a replication.

Company's inspiration
came from motivation
wanting alteration
and reconsideration
so offers an explanation
of mediation.

Lack of education
leads to toleration,
and temptation.

Now has obligation
of reformation
to protect the nation
from the mutation
by means of expiration
for the duration.

Quotation
is "Degradation
only estimation
is isolation,

amputation,
and liquidation
by strangulation
for our generation".

Validation
for the calculation
from the affirmation
caused relaxation
for the population.

Too bad this is fabrication
of visitation
for simulation.

MIL KILL
Written by Matthew Grunder
January 11, 2011

I'm in the mil
climbing over the hill
in Brazil
watching everyone kill
of their own free will,
like it's a drill.
Farmers' can't till;
instead swim like they have gills.
It makes me so ill
on how others get a thrill.
It gives me a chill.
I wish could do more than stand still.
These guys need to use their dollar bill
to buy some type of pill,
instead of trying to get their fill
by watching blood spill.
I hear a shrill.
Where's Jill?

WHERE AM I
Written by Matthew Grunder
January 23, 2013

I saw that frown on your face.
Don't let your personality go to waste.
Turn that frown upside down
into a smile.
You're standing next to the Nile.
Won't you stay awhile,
looking over the rivers, oceans, and sea?
In the Navy,
is there anywhere else you'd rather be?
A prison guard,
working hard
to prevent the fight
and help the inmates do what's right.
While also in the reserve
I'm helping all my friends
getting the answers they deserve,
but this is not the end.
Where am I?
Looking into the sky,
and trying to figure out my fate.
This makes me cry,
but I'll have to wait.

MY RELATIONSHIP

written By Matthew Grunder
May 5, 2013

Went on a trip
on a ship
and ended up in a relationship.
Started with lust
and never gained communication nor trust.
Almost makes you want to cuss,
but there's no fuss.
Oh how I adore
all the fun on the floor.
Wish we had sparked something more.
No need to be blue,
and you're laughing because this is true.
Is it something I said?
Get out of bed,
it's your dinner time. Are you fed?
It had to end,
but your still my friend.

THE SCOPE OF LIFE

Written by Matthew Grunder
March 5, 2014

What's Life all about?
I can't figure it out.

If I had the facts,
I could relax.

Let me see...
It's about who I want to be.

How do I get there from here?
Where are the answers and why aren't they clear?

Get in the car
and travel far.

Put on the brakes,
learn from, and avoid life's mistakes.

Go to college
and learn some knowledge.

Get out and about.
Go to Gold's gym and work out.

Don't be late
for a date.

Earn some money
to spend on your honey.

Pray for your sin,
so evil doesn't win.

Propose to your spouse
and buy a house.

Goals, hobbies, and dreams will inspire
you to reach your heart's desire.

The future will be bright
if you keep all these things in sight.

Where there is confusion there is hope.
So remember life's scope.

UPLIFTING HOPE

Written by Matthew Grunder
September 3, 2015

Where there's a will, there's a way.
Walk down the path I say.
The stronger the hate
the brighter the light.
A fight
goes down tonight.
It's not too late to be brave.
Save
the people from the pain.
Rain
will wash the lands suffering away.
We all pray for peace
Darkness is released.

CHANCE FOR A DATE

Written by Matthew Grunder
October 21, 2015

I tried to date
a girl named Kate.
We were supposed to go roller skate
She calls me on the phone,
and started to moan....
"The last guy wanted sex,
and started to flex.
How do I know you won't do the same?"
I said "That's lame.
Give me a chance,
and by the end of the night, we'll dance.
Let's go on a date.
It's not too late.
It might be fate."

MIGRAINE
Written by Matthew Grunder
April 1, 2016

I was in Fort Wayne
heading to Bahrain,
when I tripped, sprained
my leg, and bumped my head hurting my brain.
I was in such pain,
covered in red bloodstains.
I missed my military jet plane,
and it started to rain
causing a hurricane
in the floodplain.
John McClane
was deciding to get me to a hospital by a railroad train,
airplane,
or by an ambulance on the street in the fast lane.
A doctor explained
that I bust a vein
on the left brain,
where the connection to my membrane
resides. I felt insane.
Later I obtained
medicine to contain
my migraine.
Would you like to hear the story again?

DETERMINATE THE DEBATE

Written by Matthew Grunder
September 11, 2016

My friends work for the state,
think it's too late
to communicate
on how to operate,
and begin to speculate,
because they can't cooperate.
Treat each other like inmates,
and can't contemplate
a place to facilitate,
so they can premeditate.
All they do is play checkmate,
escalate
hate,
complicate,
irritate,
increase heart rate,
can't concentrate,
discriminate,
frustrate,
and attempt to terminate
the other all over a debate.
How much can they tolerate?
Delegate
or nominate
a third party to locate
a way to motivate,
and deviate

from pain. Participate
and elaborate
on the issues. Exterminate
the differences. Accelerate
the future to await
for something great
to determinate
at west gate.
Reintegrate
Congratulate.

ADVICE
Written by Matthew Grunder
September 11, 2016

I give advice
to girls and guys
outside under the skies
until sunrise
in my levis
and a collared shirt with one of my neckties.
I don't criticize,
or jeopardize
the problem. Answers start with verbalize.
Fear of the unknown only magnifies
and terrifies
us to where we fell paralyze.
Let out some cries.
Organize
your thoughts, I sympathize,
and empathize
with your pain. I realize
multiple solutions to justify
your problem. Satisfy
the ears as you are eating your pecan pies.

THE WHITE KNIGHT'S FIGHT

Written by Matthew Grunder
September 29, 2016

Try as I might,
to eliminate my stage freight,
fulfill my appetite.
Go out tonight,
and use my height
as the white knight
to prevent and protect others from fights.
and disasters. Fire ignites
under the starlight,
as everyone is in bed before midnight.
Save the building site
website's
communication satellite
that transmits in gigabytes
information about oncoming kryptonite
meteorites.
Superman is nowhere in flight.
Expedite
a solution. No overexcite.
Everything is just right.

TO WORK IN GRAY
Written by Matthew Grunder
October 6, 2016

My friend Allan Galloway,
and I graduated in gray
in May,
2012. Inmates are classified by age, height, and how much they
weigh.
We were taught to take away
any contraband. Spray
when necessary. Look for horseplay.
Don't let inmates block any doorways.
Know the rules and give no leeway.
Example: Level 2.0: 24.0 Refusal to obey
any lawful direct orders I say.
No inmates fall into decay.
All foods will stay
in the tray
until it's consumed by the individual or thrown away.
No buffet.
There's no such thing as a friendly friday.
TV's in cell block will display
a majority vote of football replays.
Offenders have a variety of ways
to worship and pray.
Everyday
we leave our driveways,
to get on the highway
toward our units for the public to shout "Hooray!"

THE RENAME GAME
Written by Matthew Grunder
October 19, 2016

Everything is the same
before a company goes up in flames.
They hide their shame
by playing a game
to rename.
Aim
a message to explain
to the CEO to proclaim
better companies disclaim
notice. Surprisingly no one thinks this is lame.
The new company name
gains popularity and fame.

I DO

Written by Matthew Grunder
October 22, 2016

All through
life I knew
I had to
review
my personality to pursue
my wedding day debut,
and say I do.
I had no clue,
but knew
that this was the glue.
I had a breakthrough.
I went on yahoo
and typed some searches in the queue
to view.
I needed a break, and ate barbecue,
fondue,
honeydew,
and cashews.
I'm surprised I didn't get the stomach flu.
I pondered more while playing horseshoes.
I've wanted to outdo
others. The right time to purpose is on a canoe.
I will tell her I love you.
During wedding plans, she'll find something blue.
Years down the road we'll both need a tissue.
I just want to kiss you.

HOW DID I GET HERE

Written by Matthew Grunder
March 11, 2017

Dear
my peers,
lend me your ears
to listen to a story about my years,
explaining how I got here.
My dad and uncle took me deer
hunting. In Geometry, I learned about spheres
and other shapes. 911 was causing fear
so I volunteered
12 years
in the US NAVY. I had to adhere
to UCMJ, put on headgear,
and walk on the pier
hauling military gear.
My mother had tears.
The military base showed free movie premieres.
Dad started receiving gas well paychecks from Pioneer.
I decided after 4 years
of active duty to make a new career
being a cashier
selling beer
while going to college. Sincerely
Matthew Grunder

JAILBREAK ESCAPE

Written by Matthew Grunder
March 15, 2017

Newsbreak,
two inmates Jake,
and Drake
made a jailbreak
escape
during intake
by running past a rattlesnake
during an earthquake.
Officers made a mistake
by not staying awake
and are flakes
to enforcing policy because they have headaches,
backaches,
earaches,
and toothaches.
By daybreak
the two made it to Saxet Lake
with Salisbury steaks,
cheesecakes,
and milkshakes.
But their break
ended as they were caught and forced to eat pancakes.

POWER RANGERS

Written by Matthew Grunder
March 23, 2017

The 5 Power Rangers
are teenagers
that help strangers
who are in endanger
of danger
in Angel
Grove, and work on their college major.
Don't call the operator.
Alpha 5 sends out a signal to the wristwatch communicator
to go off like a pager.
Teleport. Zordon explains the situation in the command chamber.
Solving the problem becomes a no brainier.
Get the green ranger to be a traitor
to Rita Repulsa. Cary on the remainder
of the day with confidence there is no greater
force of good. Rangers depart. Later

WHO'S GOT THE ISSUE?

Written by Matthew Grunder
April 6, 2017

A small preview
of a week ago. What to
do
with the issue
between me and you?
How do we get unstuck from the glue?
I have no clue.
Two
points of view
to
review.
A walk in each other's shoes
while listening to
Blink 182.
Who
goes first? Somewhere in the middle is something true.
Give respect and talk through
the drama. Undue
the damage. Renew
friendship. Fixed out the blue.
Thank you.

QUEST TO BE THE BEST

Written by Matthew Grunder
April 8, 2017

No. I'm not under arrest
nor is this a test,
but I've confessed
to get something off my chest.
Take off that bulletproof vest.
This might be hard to digest.
I live in the southwest
Texas and I'm on a quest
to improve my family crest
by being the best
at writing poetry. Who would have guessed
that a little time to invest
has helped expressed
ideas and stories. I have progressed
so much and I'm blessed
with this jest.
I'm glad to have addressed
you. Would you like to suggest
or request
a poem idea or story? Know that I'm not obsessed
and it will take time. Tell me if you're impressed.

STRONG SOUL
Written by Matthew Grunder
April 12, 2017

What doesn't kill you,
will make you stronger.
Be the few
to last a little longer.
Get rid of doubt.
Sink or swim?
You know what you're all about.
Go out on a whim
Take a guess.
A choice to make.
Relieve your stress.
Don't be fake.
Listen to your heart.
What does it say?
"Your smart
and you'll make it through this day."
Believe
you will reach your goal.
Achieved
to satisfy the soul.

MATT AND MEGHAN
Written by Matthew Grunder
April 12, 2017

Meghan was a saxophone musician,
who was paying tuition
at A&M Kingsville to go through several editions
of books on nutrition.
She got tired of working for Cut Co on commission.
Her brother Matt continued the tradition
of joining the US Navy on missions
hauling ammunition.
Later he became an information system technician
who learned how to position
military satellites, thus achieving transmission.
Meghan and Matt would relax by getting admission
to six Flags Fiesta Texas where they heard R Kelly Ignition.
Matt's time in the US Navy was up and stayed only on one condition.
Join NMCB-22 in the US Navy reserves working on demolition.
Both Matt and Meghan achieved their ambitions.

LOVE DANCE

Written by Matthew Grunder
April 15, 2017

Dance
Like no one is watching.
Find romance,
instead of walking
away from what could have been.
You're good
at everything else but when
and how you should
date.
Sometimes you want advice.
However, you found the time to wait
and look into the eyes
of your one true
love.
You knew
your prayer would be answered from above.
All
you had to do was find a connection.
Fall
in love to get affection.
With this ring,
I will be wed.
To her, I'll bring
anything to keep out of sickness and in bed.

RARE BREED

written by Matthew Grunder
May 17, 2017

I am a rare breed
that will take the lead
so others will follow and proceed
with speed
to do good deeds.
I am the one who freed
them from others greed,
taught them to plant seeds
with their steeds,
taught others to read,
play the reed,
and meet other needs.
Choose your creed.
I plead
with you to exceed
so that you will succeed.
Indeed.

COMPLETE ULTIMATE ATHLETE

Written by Matthew Grunder
May 28, 2017

I am an athlete
who never cheats,
and loves to compete
against the elite
Ultimate Frisbee team fleet.
To beat
and defeat
my competition: I eat
the right foods, delete
the junk foods, use my gym worksheet
to repeat
the exercises, and run in my cleats
on the streets.
till my feet
get swole. My training is complete.

THE NIGHT AT ODORI NIGHTCLUB

Written by Matthew Grunder
May 31, 2017

I am single
and looking to mingle
so one night I went to Odori Nightclub
to get some pub.
Saw a girl
and decided to give it a whirl.
I approached her started to talk
our eyes started to interlock
as I said "Hello
show
me your dance
moves." She took a chance
with me and we both started to smile.
We ended up dating for a while.
I loved the way we kissed.
I did not miss
the day we got married.
I carried
my spouse
across the threshold into our house.

THE TASK AT HAND

Written by Matthew Grunder
June 4, 2017

Focus on the task
at hand.
Take off your mask
of confusion to understand
the issue
that caused the block out.
Get a tissue
and give a shout out.
Pray
to learn the skills
that someday
will
light
a path,
make everything alright,
and get rid of doubt's wrath.
Fear
is something you can expect.
Let me make it clear.
You must protect
yourself
from worry.
Be oneself
and don't hurry.

NO MORE

written by Matthew Grunder
June 22, 2017

It's strange
how things change.
We are in danger
of how we treat a complete stranger.
Some people are victims of use
and abuse.
I can't ignore
it. No more.
Can't we get along
and stop doing what's wrong?
This world is so corrupt,
but know that I'm not giving up.
We can each
reach
a place in our heart to find
a way to be kind.
Think of
love
and cast everything aside.
Let your conscience be your guide.
It's not too late
to let get rid of hate
and forget
that mindset.
Forgive
those that have caused you pain and live
your life a better way. Let it end
with us being friends.

WHO IS GOD?

Written by Matthew Grunder
July 2, 2017

God is able
to teach a man to fish to provide food at the table.
None of God's stories are fables.
God is good
and would
want you to follow and listen well into your adulthood.
God is great.
Get rid of hate.
Do good deeds, help others, and lending some money are ways to
donate.
God is powerful
and merciful.
Do the right thing and be cheerful.
From the beginning
eating
the fruit from the tree of knowledge was the only thing that was
forbidden.
God was forgiving.
God is loving
and trusting.
He is coming
to judge the living
and the dead.
God will bring
happiness to your life and help you with anything.
God is everything.

JESUS' UPLIFTING HOPE

written by Matthew Grunder
August 5, 2017

Where there's a will there's a way.
Walk down the chosen path… I say.
The stronger the hate,
the brighter the light.
A fight
to make things right
goes down tonight.
It's not too late
to be brave,
take a stand,
and take Jesus' hand.
Save
the people from every possible pain.
Rain
will wash all the lands suffering away.
We all pray:
"In Jesus' name I
revoke all evil spirits
and demons. I bind
all your powers and
cast all of you back
to hell in Jesus' name."
for peace.
Darkness is released.
All acts of evil will cease.

RISING PROBLEMS

written by Matthew Grunder
September 20, 2017

My eyes
have seen so many problems rise
to the top.
It's up to me to put a stop
to and tell others about my contributions.
I have several solutions.
Use all available resources
to stay on course.
Go into the field
to shield
innocent bystanders from the disaster.
Send a response team to aid in recovering faster.
It doesn't matter whenever,
or whatever
the problem occurred.
Rest assured
it will be resolved.
We will look around
until all the answers are found.

THE DEFENDER

written by Matthew Grunder
October 3, 2017

I am a defender
that will never surrender.
I say it loud
and proud
with all my might,
"I'm ready to fight
on offense,
or defense."
The victims that are under attack
are ready to get their lives back.
It's time
to analyze the crime.
I will collect
evidence to build a suspect.
Turn it over to the police, DA, judge, and lawyers to prepare
a fair
trial, to avoid double
jeopardy against the criminal that caused so much trouble.
I am a hero
that turned a criminal into a zero.
Also, I'm the man
with a plan.

LIES

written by Matthew Grunder
January 21, 2018

Why do people lie
to get by
and have their way.
Trying to get everyone to believe what they say.
Why live in sin
just to win?
Some people have no clue
that person has issues.
A walk-in another's shoes is a must.
Reintegrate respect, friendship, and trust.
Do the right thing from the start
and listen to your heart.
If you let the world of truth and lies collide
it will eat you up inside.
Take my hand
and let's pray to help you understand.
From this point forward: do what is fair
and take care.

BODYBUILDING

written by Matthew Grunder
July 28, 2018

Lifting weights
before dates
will create
muscle if performed
with form.
I will consider
being a bodybuilder
and improving my diet.
Time to try it.
I'm going to bulk
to become the next Incredible Hulk.
The jet fit app
will log my resting gaps,
track
my back,
triceps,
biceps,
chest,
other muscle groups, and allow me to test
my weight limits. If you're not hardcore,
leave. There's the door.
I'm about
a great workout.
Yes!
I made progress.
In conclusion
muscle confusion
should be part of your workout routine.
Remember to eat protein.
Exercise
will increase your body's size.

THOUGHTS OF LIFE

Written by Matthew Grunder
October 24, 2018

My thoughts
of life
have brought
me a wife.
I'm thankful for doing good deeds
and charity.
It has allowed me to proceed
with clarity,
and end
confusion.
I will protect
my family and friends
from fear's
illusions.
I hear
the sound
of God's voice.
He tells
me not to neglect
or forsake his people from the seven deadly sins of hell.
Always around
to make the right
choice
to save their soul,
and show them how to set goals.
Bring you into the light
to accomplish your hopes and dreams.
Father forgive all evil acts and thoughts with some screams.

RIGHT MY WRONGS

written by Matthew Grunder
April 26, 2019

We are all capable of right and wrong,
but must find a way to get along
and gain a sense of belonging
in the community.
We all have the opportunity
to find unity,
to befriend
complete strangers, recommend
advice, and attend
church,
research
bible scriptures, and search
for God.
Start by defrauding
your life. Time to applaud
you for doing what's right.
Tonight
the light
shines grace.
You have erased
your wrongs and earned a place
in heaven.

RECEIVE LOVE

Written by Matthew Grunder
June 8, 2019

Inspired by:
The Lord is close to the brokenhearted and saves those who are crushed in spirit.
PSLAM 34:18

The wound of rejection is slow to heal.
My heart has been corrupted
with unfaithfulness replaced
love and has a seal
on a heart.
Here's how the story starts....
Men bury the pain of rejection
and act like they need no protection.
So many questions of doubt
have a man's mind racing all about.
Why doesn't my wife
love me?
If she
doesn't want me, who would?
Could
this be the end of my life?
Is it right for a spouse to have extramarital affair?
On the day of the wedding, the couple shared
love and spiritual connection.
Woke up one day and one had a reflection.
This isn't the way one wanted life to be.
I'll just pack and flee.
God's love for you is strong
and he will help you along
your way
any day.
That's a promise that is never spoken.
No words exchanged and never broken.

LEAP OF FAITH
written by Matthew Grunder
June 16, 2019

Leaping for my faith.
Looking for the right answers.
Guided by God's angels.

MY THIRD EYE

written by Matthew Grunder
August 3, 2019

I've got a thirst
to be first
in my profession
asking all the right questions.
I'm going to do my part
and start
with my third eye
asking why.
Trust my gut
to know what
happened. Use context clues
to know who
done it. Where
did you get scared?
The most interesting is how.
All I can say is "wow."
Then
comes when
I took
a look
on several ebooks
for information
on that computer workstation.
I want the answer
for the cure of cancer.
Explore
all the possibilities and keep looking for more.
Let me conclude
with gratitude.

LOST SOUL
written by Matthew Grunder
October 14, 2019

There was a man
named Noah who was lost
and ran
from his first marriage.
He thought everything was nice and sound
when he found
a crazy
lazy
woman named Lilith with six baby carriages.
She gets a thrill
by telling her kids to kill
themselves. The confused
man had no clue
of what leaving a good marriage costs.
He would be used
and abused
for affection
all through
life
by his new wife
when there's no real connection.
Lilith wanted a life insurance policy
on Noah, but he honestly
refused.
She can be so cruel
when it comes to enforcing her husband's rules.
Noah be brave
and save
yourself from this nightmare
with a prayer.

DEBT
Written by Matthew Grunder
October 22, 2019

I'm a military cadet
that lost a bet
at sunset,
and ended up in debt.
I haven't learned my lesson yet.
Now I lost my safety net,
and assets.
I'm upset.
Let me have a cigarette
to forget
I can't afford an omelet,
or internet.
I regret
selling my television set,
and clarinet.
I can't take a shower to get wet
after sweating.
I can't take Juliet
on a date. I need an outlet
for fun. Time to reset.

PRAYER

written by Matthew Grunder
October 25, 2019

You put all
your hope
and dreams
in prayer
to call
forth God's grand design
scheme
to help share
the good news,
and shine
blessed
grace.
Let's
cope
with the stressed
disciples, and choose
right over wrong
to erase
sin.
It won't be long
for good to prevail and win.

UNDERSTAND
written by Matthew Grunder
October 25, 2019

I've planned
all my life and there are things I don't understand.
Is insurance
around to give us assurance?
Why do we need math
formulas to show us the path,
so that we could
cut some wood?
Why do we need
to read?
Never cross
your boss
especially during an interview
for it is their point of view
that matter
and decide if you go up the career ladder.
So many things left to explain
that still
remain.
I need to get my fill.
It's my role
to play by ear
and not let fear
control
me.
I see
the way
today.

WAITING

written by Matthew Grunder
November 7, 2019

So many things in life I've been waiting for.
An opportunity opened the door
to find so much more
when I explore.
I took a vacation
to end my frustration,
admire all of creation,
while listening to my favorite radio station.
All of
my life I've been looking for love
in the wrong places. Push comes to shove
I want a woman to think of
life with. You're a life saver
by doing me a favor.
I get to savor
your cooked foods flavor.
Devise
a way using my eyes
to see through disguises
and be very wise.

WHY AM I LIKE THIS?

written by Matthew Grunder
February 11, 2020

I can't dismiss,
why am I like this?
very strong.
Love singing karaoke songs.
My life is tragic
It's as if everything happens by magic.
Move towards
my goals and earn rewards.
Stand apart
from the crowd being smart.
Start
the day with a kind heart.
Be brave
till my grave.
I took an ASVAB test
to discover I'm the best.
Let us give thanks
for me joining the military ranks.

MISTAKES
Written by Matthew Grunder
December 21, 2020

Take a break
from mistakes.
Don't cheat
so you won't end up on the street.
End all the lies
with some cries.
I won't offend
my friendship to the end.
Don't fuss
or cuss.
I couldn't ask for more
than to prevent war.
Give hugs
instead of doing drugs.
Be real
and don't steal.
Have fun
instead of shooting others with a gun.
I need a shrink
to talk about my problems and drinks.
How about a toast
to what I dream of most.
Have a bright
future so everything's alright.

STAND DOWN

written by Matthew Grunder
May 27, 2021

Stand down.
For Jesus Christ wore the crown
of thorns. End
the fight
between evil, and good.
Spend
time at church. Shine
in the light.
Could
you turn water into wine?
Clean
your soul.
Let that be your goal.
Pray
everyday
for anything
and everything.
Tonight
I advise
you, it's your night
to rise
and carry
your cross. Sing to Mary.
Blessed be
it's about the good person I want to be.

GAY OR BI
written by Matthew Grunder
June 22, 2021

Sometimes I'm gay
and sometimes I'm bi.
I try
to go about my day
with LGBT pride.
I don't want to hide
no more.
Hear
me roar
with no fear.
No longer will I cry.
I'm tired of asking why
I'm like this.
I want my first kiss.
I don't care what you think.
Tough men wear pink.
Wink!
Give me a chance
for some romance.

CUERO GOBBLER FOOTBALL
written by Matthew Grunder
March 11, 2022

Go go
Cuero Gobblers. You are all
football
player
pros,
who need a prayer.
You fight
on offense,
and defense
tonight.
Rain, sleet, or snow
the quarterback
leads the pack
and throws
to the bros.
The next play
to make your day
is a kickoff
from the tee
a handoff
and taking a knee.
There nothing more
exciting than a tie.
The playoff high
score
will mean war
For
your information the Cuero Gobblers won.
The football game is done.

Printed in the United States
by Baker & Taylor Publisher Services